I SPY
UP IN THE SKY

THE STARS

BY
TAMRA ORR

Mitchell Lane
PUBLISHERS

P.O. Box 196
Hockessin, Delaware 19707
Visit us on the web: www.mitchelllane.com
Comments? email us:
mitchelllane@mitchelllane.com

The Clouds
The Moon
The Stars
The Sun

Printing   1   2   3   4   5   6   7   8   9

ABOUT THE AUTHOR: Award-winning children's book author Tamra Orr lives with her family in the Pacific Northwest.

Library of Congress Cataloging-in-Publication Data
Orr, Tamra.
I spy up in the sky the stars / by Tamra Orr.
    p. cm. — (Randy's corner: I spy up in the sky...)
Includes bibliographical references and index.
ISBN 978-1-58415-975-9 (library bound)
1. Stars—Juvenile literature. I. Title.
QB801.7.O67 2011
523.8—dc22
                                                                                    2011000783

eBook ISBN: 9781612281452

                                                                                    PLB

THE
STARS

When the Sun goes down
And fades out of sight,
Darkness arrives,
Revealing starlight.

In the night sky
Stars twinkle and glow,
Born in the big bang
Billions of years ago.

Full of hydrogen, helium,
And other gases,
Stars form galaxies
When they cluster in masses.

Our Sun's galaxy
Is the Milky Way
With billions of stars—
A spiral on display.

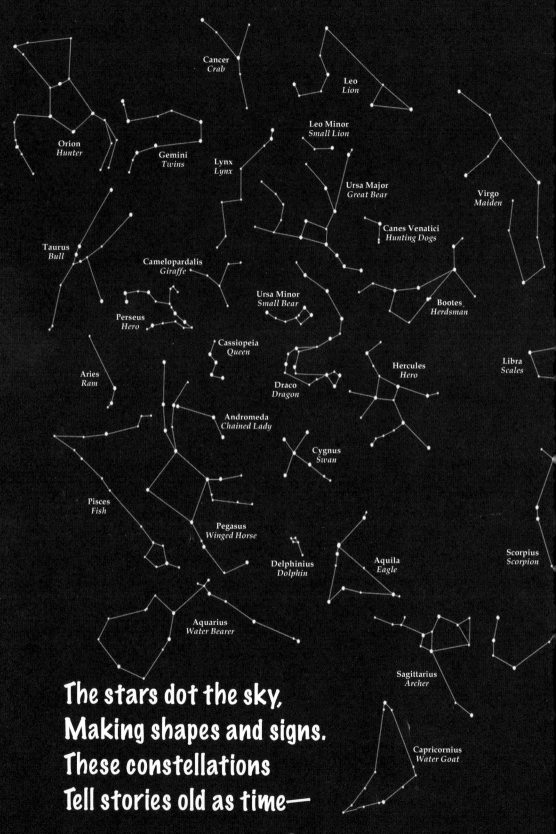

Cancer
Crab

Leo
Lion

Leo Minor
Small Lion

Orion
Hunter

Gemini
Twins

Lynx
Lynx

Ursa Major
Great Bear

Virgo
Maiden

Canes Venatici
Hunting Dogs

Taurus
Bull

Camelopardalis
Giraffe

Ursa Minor
Small Bear

Bootes
Herdsman

Perseus
Hero

Cassiopeia
Queen

Draco
Dragon

Hercules
Hero

Libra
Scales

Aries
Ram

Andromeda
Chained Lady

Cygnus
Swan

Pisces
Fish

Pegasus
Winged Horse

Delphinius
Dolphin

Aquila
Eagle

Scorpius
Scorpion

Aquarius
Water Bearer

Sagittarius
Archer

Capricornius
Water Goat

The stars dot the sky,
Making shapes and signs.
These constellations
Tell stories old as time—

8

Stories of heroes,
Legends looking down,
Quietly watching
Those still on the ground.

Stars are described
By heat, color, and size.
Some are small and dim;
Some are clear to the eyes.

Flame Nebula

Class O stars are rare,
Burning blue and strong—
Hotter than a million Suns,
They don't live very long.

Alnitak

Class B stars are bright
And often come in pairs.
These binary stars
The same orbit share.

Sometimes these groups have
Many more, it's true.
The Pleiades count
Seven Sisters plus two.

Alcyone

Pleione

Atlas

Asterope

Taygete

Maia

Celaene

Electra

Merope

THE PLEIADES (SEVEN SISTERS) AND
THEIR PARENTS, ATLAS AND PLEIONE

SUMMER TRIANGLE

Vega (Class A)

Deneb
(Supergiant)

Altair
(Class A)

The simple white stars
That are part of class A
Are not unusual
In the Milky Way.

14

Milky Way

Altair and Vega
Are extremely white.
Not far from Earth,
They light up the night.

As for class F stars,
All across the sky—
A simple telescope
Can help identify.

North Star
(Polaris)

The tail of Ursa Minor
Is the bright North Star.
It has guided many sailors
From near and afar.

Pherkad

Anwar al Farkadain

Kochab

Alifa al Farkadain

Epsilon

Ursa Minor
(Little Bear)

Yildun

Polaris

Supergiant stars
Are part of class G.
They burn very bright,
And are easy to see.

Earth's Sun is a G.
It is yellow-white.
It warms the planet
With rays of sunlight.

Sun

Aldebaran

Class K stars are cooler,
Orange to the eye.
They're still some of the
Brightest in the sky.

Constellation Taurus
Has a star from class K.
Called Aldebaran, it's
Sixty-five light-years away.

Class M stars are common
They're everywhere.
In both mass and size,
No others can compare.

Antares

In the group Orion,
Betelgeuse is one.
So is bright Antares
In the Scorpion.

Stars live a long time
Before they begin to die.
They burn out slowly
Before saying good-bye.

LIFE CYCLE OF A STAR

Bigger star grows,
cools, and turns red

Nuclear reactions
cause star to make
light and heat

SUPERGIANT

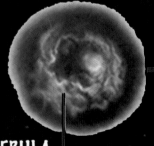

RED GIANT

NEBULA

**MAIN-
SEQUENCE
STAR**

Thick part in
nebula starts to
shrink and warm up

Smaller star
grows and glows
red as it cools

Now and then a star
Explodes with bright light
This is called a nova—
An incredible sight.

Supergiant explodes

Center collapses
and becomes thick

SUPERNOVA

NEUTRON STAR

Center collapses
and disappears

BLACK HOLE

Hot center becomes
white dwarf

Outer layers
of gas
puff off

Star cools
and becomes red

Star stops
glowing

 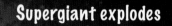

PLANETARY
NEBULA

WHITE
DWARF

WHITE
DWARF
COOLING

BLACK
DWARF

With a supernova,
A star explodes and flares,
Collapsing on itself,
Getting denser there.

Shockwaves ripple out,
From which new stars are made.
A neutron star is born,
And a nebula's displayed.

Horsehead
Nebula

If you look up and see
A shooting star go by,
Leaving a path of light
As it streaks across the sky,

It is a meteor—
Not a star at all.
Stars burn and explode,
But they never fall.

Star Facts

Stars form from mainly hydrogen gas and dust.

Stars give off huge amounts of energy (heat and light). Class O stars are the hottest.

Our Sun is a medium-sized class G star. It is about 93 million miles (150 million kilometers) from Earth.

The next closest star, Promixa Centauri, is about 23.5 trillion miles (38 trillion kilometers, or 4.2 light-years) away.

On a clear night, without using a telescope, you can see about 3,000 stars.

Star Classes

Class	Color	Example
O	Blue	Alnitak (Zeta Orionis)
B	Blue	Pleiades
A	White	Vega, Altair
F	White or yellow	Polaris (North star)
G	Yellow	Earth's Sun
K	Orange	Aldebaran
M	Red	Betelgeuse, Antares

GLOSSARY

Aldebaran (al-deh-BAYR-on) — An orange giant star that marks the eye of Taurus, the bull constellation.

Antares (an-TAR-eez) — A red supergiant star in the constellation Scorpius (the Scorpion).

Betelgeuse (BEE-tul-joos) — The second brightest star in the constellation Orion.

Big Bang — The idea that the universe began with a huge explosion of energy.

binary (BY-nayr-ee) **stars** — A pair of stars that revolve around a common center of gravity.

black dwarf — A star at the end of its life, when it has cooled too much to produce heat or light.

black hole — A region of space that has so much gravity, nothing can escape it, not even light. Scientists believe a black hole is left when a massive star collapses.

constellation (kon-stel-AY-shun) — A group of stars that ancient people saw as pictures.

galaxy (GAA-lak-zee) — A very large group of stars and other space matter.

gravity (GRAA-vih-tee) — A force that acts on all matter in the universe, causing objects to pull on one another. It is the force that keeps objects on Earth from floating into space.

helium (HEE-lee-um) — A lightweight, colorless element that is usually in the form of gas.

hydrogen (HY-droh-jen) — A colorless, odorless element that is usually in the form of gas. It is one of the two ingredients that make up water.

light-year — The distance light travels in one year (about 5.88 trillion miles, or 9.46 trillion kilometers).

mass — The amount of matter in an object.

meteor (MEE-tee-or) — A small, solid body from space that hits Earth's atmosphere.

nebula (NEH-byoo-luh) — A cloud of dust and gas; the plural is *nebulae* (NEH-byoo-lee).

neutron (NOO-tron) **star** — A very dense object that is made when a large star collapses.

nova (NOH-vuh) — A star that ejects some of its material and becomes brighter in the process.

orbit — The usually oval path that one body in space takes around another body in space.

Orion (oh-RY-un) — A large, bright constellation that ancient people named for a great hunter; there are three bright stars in Orion's belt, and the bright red star Betelgeuse marks his shoulder.

Pleiades (PLEE-uh-deez) — A group of seven stars in the constellation Taurus, named for the seven daughters of Atlas and Pleione (PLEE-oh-nee).

Polaris (poh-LAYR-is) — The North Star, it is the star directly above the sky's North Pole.

supergiant (SOO-per-jy-unt) — An extremely bright star of a very large diameter and low mass.

supernova (SOO-per-noh-vuh) — A star that exploded and has become extremely bright.

Ursa Minor — The "Little Bear" constellation, also known as the Little Dipper. The end of the bear's tail (the dipper's handle) is Polaris.

FURTHER READING

Works Consulted

Atlas of the Universe: Classification of Stars. http://www.atlasofthe universe.com/startype.html

"Binary Star Explosion Inside Nebula Challenges Star Theory." *ScienceDaily* , November 25, 2008. http://www.sciencedaily.com/ releases/2008/11/081119084533.htm

NASA's Imagine the Universe! http:// imagine.gsfc.nasa.gov/index.html

Notable Nearby Stars. http://www. solstation.com/stars.htm

SkyEye: 88 Constellations. http:// www.obliquity.com/skyeye/ 88const/

Stellar Alchemy: Properties of Stars. http://geology.csupomona.edu/ janourseCosmicPerspectiveXtra Chapters/AWL_Bennett_Ch16.pdf

The Universe Today: Stars. http:// www.universetoday.com/24184/ stars/

Books

Fuerst, Jeffrey. *Star Light, Star Bright*. New York: Newmark Learning, 2010.

James, Lincoln. *The Sun: Star of the Solar System*. New York: Gareth Stevens Publishing, 2010.

Mitton, Jacqueline. *Zoo in the Sky: A Book of Animal Constellations*. Washington, DC: National Geographic Children's Books, 2006.

Purslow, Frances. *Constellations*. New York: Weigl Publishers, 2006.

Rice, William. *Stars: Neighbors in Space*. California: Teacher Created Materials, 2010.

Simon, Seymour. *Stars*. New York: Mulberry Books, 2006.

Stott, Carole. *I Wonder Why Stars Twinkle*. New York: Kingfisher, 2011.

On the Internet

Astronomy for Kids: Stars http://www.kidsastronomy.com/ stars.htm

Cosmos4Kids!: Stars http://www.cosmos4kids.com/ files/stars_intro.html

The Space Place: Make a Star Finder http://spaceplace.nasa.gov/en/ kids/st6starfinder/st6starfinder. shtml

INDEX